A Pictorial History of Austin, Minnesota
VOLUME III
Presented by the Austin Daily Herald

Copyright© 2002 • ISBN: 1-932129-31-6
All rights reserved. No part of this book may be reproduced, stored in a retrieval system or transmitted in any form or by any means, electronic, mechanical, photocopying, recording or otherwise, without prior written permission of the copyright owner or the publisher.
Published by Pediment Publishing, a division of The Pediment Group, Inc. www.pediment.com

Table of Contents

Foreword 4

Commerce 5

Public Service 19

Industry 39

Schools & Churches 48

Sports & Leisure 69

Disasters 93

Labor 100

Community 105

Foreword

During the past seven years the *Austin Daily Herald*, working with our partner the Mower County Historical Society, has worked to produce a photographic history of the Austin community. With this book we have completed our work and assembled a trilogy that all living here, or who have lived here, should have.

The trilogy documents not only a community's history, but perhaps more importantly details a community's continuing progress. Austin, Minnesota, has faced its share of disasters and discord and met it with a determination to grow, to prosper and to build a better community.

This book is the third volume of *A Pictorial History of Austin, Minnesota,* and depicts life in Austin from the late 1960s through present day. The second volume captured the years from the 1940s to the 1970s and the first volume covered life in the 1800s up through the 1930s.

As with the first two volumes, volume three would not have been possible without the help of the Mower County Historical Society and its fine staff and volunteers. The photos portrayed in this book are mainly from the archives of the *Austin Daily Herald*, but do include some from the Historical Society's archives.

Assembly of this book and arrangements for printing and binding were handled with professional skill by Bill Adams and Brad Fenison of Pediment Publishing, Vancouver, Washington.

This book is dedicated to all those who have ties to Austin, Minnesota, and who have left our community steeped in history and richly blessed.

Neal Ronquist
Publisher, Austin Daily Herald

Commerce

The changing face of Austin, and time, is best illustrated in the businesses that have come and gone. While the backbone of Austin's vibrant economy remains agriculture and the Hormel Foods, Corp., the small business landscape has changed to reflect new technologies and the need for new services.

Throughout the 1970s, 1980s, 1990s, and into the new century, Austin's businesses were forced to either adapt, or die. Many have met the challenge of the new service economy and have thrived. New businesses, reflecting societies changing tastes and needs have popped up replacing antiquated businesses and shops.

Rapid changed is the hallmark of the past three decades when it comes to business and as the photos show Austin has met the challenge and continues to grow.

Dedication ceremony of the second phase of the downtown renewal project, October 1978. Left to right: Ed Smith, Housing and Redevelopment Authority commissioner; Sid Russell, HRA commissioner; Bill Hunter, Austin plant manager of the George A. Hormel & Co.; Joe Wagner, contractor for the downtown project; Mayor Robert Enright; Bud Anderson, Project Area Committee chairman; Mel Schleuder, past PAC chairman; and Ken Fossey, city councilman.

Beginning the downtown urban renewal project in the early 1970s.

The beginnings of the downtown urban renewal project which became known as the Downtown Plaza. The entire project took over five years to complete.

Construction during Phase II of the downtown urban renewal project.

Construction during Phase II of the Downtown Plaza. The project was completed and dedicated in 1978 at a cost of $324,234.

Commerce ❖ 7

Holiday Inn at 1701 14th Street NW.

Austin Area Chamber of Commerce located at 300 North Main Street.

The "Enjoy Austin" sign was dedicated by the Jaycees in 1975.

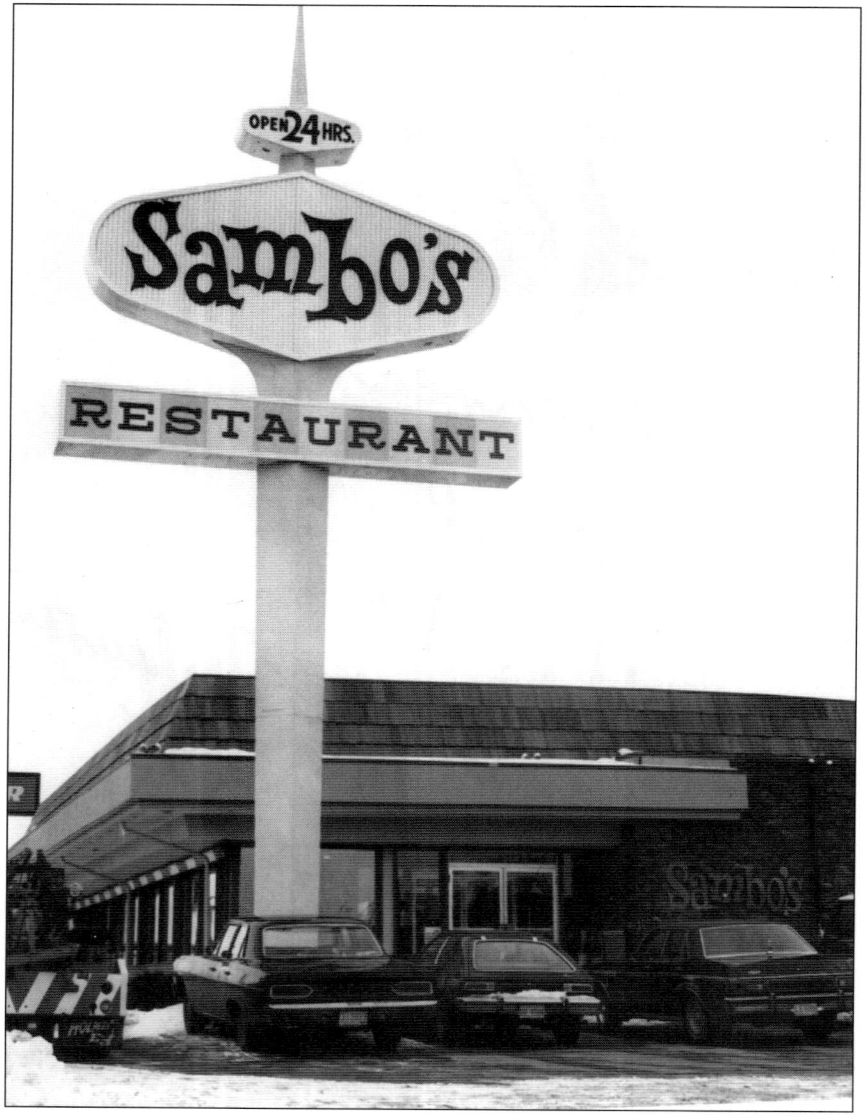

Sambo's Restaurant at 1130 North Main Street, circa 1976.

First Fidelity Bank set growth records in savings gains, mortgage lending, and asset growth in 1978.

The Serendipity at 311 North Main Street was owned by Steve and Joan Weiland in 1979.

Commerce ❖ 9

Business partners Miss Irene Taylor and Jack Konovsky announced the sale of Austin Auto Co., at 215 3rd Avenue NE, to Holiday Dodge in January 1972. Austin Auto Co. was one of the oldest car dealerships in the city.

Owners Alan Jacobson and Fran Bishop in the newly remodeled Loading Dock Lounge at 110 4th Avenue NE in March 1979.

The Fawver Agency was founded in 1969 by Charlie Fawver, March 1979.

Rosenthal's Flooring and Decorating at 610 1st Avenue SW.

Red Cedar Inn at 705 North Main Street was owned by Duane Farr in 1980.

Interior of the Norge Laundry and Cleaning Village at 1000 1st Avenue SW, owned by Stanley and Opal Sprague, 1981.

The opening of Domino's Pizza at 106 South Main Street on March 6, 1985.

Robbins furniture store at 214 1st Street NE.

Austin business leaders working to improve the city's ability to attract new business, June 1992. Left to right: City Administrator Pat McGarvey, Vice-President of CPS Maryann Bachkes, Hormel employee Rick Bross, and Mayer Funeral Home employee John Mayer, Jr.

Grand opening of Kuehn Motor in September 1992.

Clock being installed in front of Nemitz store at 407 North Main Street.

Mike and Kathy Weins, Dairy Queen owners at 1200 West Oakland Avenue in 1985.

Eastside Shopping Mall located at 104 11th Street SW.

Dolan's TrimScape landscaping center located at 411 East Oakland Avenue, circa 1993.

Workers dressed up for "Red, White, and Blue Day" at K-Mart at 1101 North Main Street in March 1991 to support people involved in Desert Storm.

KAVT-FM's station transmitter on the north side of the Austin Area Vocational Technical Institute. The station began broadcast operations in January 1981.

Cash Wise Food & Drug at 1300 18th Avenue NW, 2002.

Security State Bank at 805 North Main Street, 2002.

Commerce ❖ 15

Moving a house on Oakland Avenue West.

Johnny's Restaurant at 1130 North Main Street, circa 1990.

Main Street drug store at 1305 1st Avenue SW, 2002.

Kwik Trip gas station at 1201 West Oakland Avenue, 2002.

Wells Fargo bank at 501 North Main Street, 2002.

Target at 1701 18th Avenue NW, 2002.

Hy-Vee Food Store at 1001 18th Avenue NW, 2002.

King Buffet at 1610 17th Street NW, 2002.

The crew of Precision Signs moved the new Oak Park Mall sign into place on December 2000. The $65,000 sign structure featured a scrolling marquee and lighted CineMagic sign in addition to the mall sign.

El Mariachi Mexican Restaurant and Great Dragon Chinese restaurant at 227 and 229 Main Street North, 2002.

Hanson's Camera Shop in Oak Park Mall on 18th Avenue NW, 2002.

The Murphy Creek development project ceremoniously began on April 10, 2001, with a groundbreaking attended by many, including several ambassadors from the Chamber of Commerce. At the shovels, from left to right: Chairman of the Board, president and CEO of Hormel Foods Corporation, Joel Johnson; Jerry Anfinson of Apex Austin; President of the Hormel Foundation Richard Knowlton; MHFA Commissioner Kit Hadley; Councilwoman Gloria Nordin; developer Mike Podawiltz; Councilman-at-Large Dick Chaffee; Councilwoman Mickey Jorgenson; Mayor Bonnie Rietz; and Councilman Dick Lang.

Public Service

City Council meeting on January 5, 1981. In the background, left to right: City Engineer Dick Murphy, Mayor Robert Enright, and City Administrator-Treasurer Darrell Stacy.

Like all communities, Austin has had a need for volunteers to step forward and give of themselves for the betterment of the community.

Throughout the decades of the 1970s, 1980s and 1990s, residents of Austin heeded the call of their brethren and gave of their time to many endeavors.

Austinites have always taken their politics seriously, making candidates for offices plentiful. The crop of candidates has made elections interesting and insured all voices have been heard.

In addition, Austin is full of service clubs. The member-driven clubs provide help to those in need and aid many different causes throughout a given year.

It takes a community to raise a child and Austin has found many volunteers ready to accept the challenge and make the community a better place.

Workmen laying the concrete base of a sewer lift station at the south end of 6th Street SW in April 1967. The station would serve the newly developing areas in Austin's west section.

Austin Utilities workers performing repairs in 1969.

The Mower County Bookmobile carried 3,000 volumes and special requests for its 37 stops on a two-week schedule in 1969.

Austin Achievement Corp. changed its name to Cedar Valley Workshop in April 1967. The previous year 69 clients were served at the workshop totalling $55,000 in wages paid to them. The workshop realized approximately $138,000 income from work done by the clients. Left to right: President Amil Reed, Director Laura Zemil, Ferris Furtney, Ralph Day.

U.S. Congressman Al Quie stopped at Le Roy Bakery Cafe during a 1965 re-election campaign stop.

Phil Shealy, county planner, with one of 80 aerial view photos taken at the 1,000 foot level of Austin and Mower County used for a comprehensive land-use survey in February 1968.

Twelve women completed the fourth Home Health Aide orientation course and received their certificates and pins, 1967. Pictured: Mildred Alford, Lillian Cole, Arlene Draayer, Leona Johnson, Martha Jurgens, Catherine Norby, Ruth Fiedler, Jeanette Schmidt, Marie Schrafel, Julia Shane, Eleanor Schisler, Miriam Younker, Ann Agerbeck, and Mrs. Frederickson.

Outgoing President of the Austin Police Benefit Association John Hulet shaking hands with his successor Duane Klingerman in May 1968.

Laurel Overby distributing outgoing mail into slots at the Austin Post Office in 1966.

The Austin Public Library contained: 213,959 books, 10,322 records, 11,142 periodicals, 1,024 films, and 238 framed pictures in 1969.

Roger Plunkett making a presentation at the Austin Public Library, 1979.

Public Service ❖ 23

The nearly complete Austin Activity Center, 1971.

Building beams for the multi purpose arena in May 1973. It later became Riverside Arena.

Robert Enright, Austin Mayor from 1968-1970.

Construction of the Austin Utilities warehouse across the street from the Municipal Building in November 1976.

Riverside Arena located at 501 2nd Avenue NE, 1977.

Courthouse and Law Enforcement Center south from 2nd Avenue NE, circa 1976.

Austin Post Office at 200 1st Avenue SE, circa 1976.

Mower County Courthouse and Law Enforcement on the 100 block of Main Street looking east, 1976. The statue on the left is George Washington.

Construction of the 205 unit twin tower high rise elderly housing project at 1st Street and 1st Avenue NE in October 1978.

Austin United Way members of 1977.

Jay Best, a blood recipient, urged Mower County residents to donate at the Red Cross Bloodmobile collection, August 1979.

The United Way Board of Directors conducting its May 1977 meeting at the Red Cross building during a "working lunch" session.

The first meeting of the Advisory Energy Board at the Municipal Building in June 1978. Left to right: Chairman Ken Moen, David Kane, Vice-Chairman Janice Smaby, Vince Lynch, and secretary Ron Sala.

Members of the Austin United Way Campaign Cabinet standing in front of the goal board in the Courthouse Square after they reached their goal of $240,000 for the first time in 15 years in January 1980. Pictured are: Dr. Milt Stensland, Bill Hunter, Dr. Richard Trumble, Reverend Carl Borgwardt, Dave Wenzel, Phil Nolan, John Hanson, Jerry Anfinson, Jim Hall, Ted Colescott, Mary Frances Jones, Rich Melin, Bill Weidner, Don Sandeen, Harold Mattfeld, Jim Seeley, Oliver Herrick, Marilyn Anderson, John Lasher, Bob Brinkman, R. Forslan, M.E. Murgstahler, Bob Thatcher, Bob Fitgerald, and Arlan Burmeister.

Minnesota Governor Al Quie during his talk at St. Edwards Community Center for the "Capitol for a Day" program in November 1980.

Governor Al Quie at First Bank on November 25, 1980.

Governor Al Quie at Austin High School for the "Capitol for a Day" program on November 25, 1980.

Representatives of the agencies which donated funds to the renovation and refurbishing of a van for the Mower County chapter of the American Red Cross with the chapter chairman, 1980. The van was presented to the chapter by Northwestern Bell Telephone Company and worked on by students at the Austin Area Vocational Technical Institute. Pictured are: Charles French, Kiwanis president; Richard Henry, Early Risers Kiwanis president; Ramsey Johnson, Sertoma president; James Mittun, Lions president; Lee Littlefield, Elkto Community Club; Ruth Rasmussen, Zonta vice president; Daniel Miller, chapter chairman; Mrs. Donald Landherr, Adams American Legion Auxiliary; Robert Fitzgerald, Northwestern Bell Austin manager; Keno Knutson, Northwestern Bell regional manager; Harry Lenz, Lyle Lions president; and Fred Creighton, Rotary president.

Paging through the book signed by the people in attendance at the surprise contribution gathering at the Salvation Army on January 5, 1984.

Austin policeman Jerry Ginamit getting ready to leave on patrol.

Building the Y.M.C.A. addition in December 1981.

Nearing completion of the Y.M.C.A. addition, 1982.

St. Olaf Hospital at 101 4th Street NW on October 25, 1982.

Dick Benzkofer, City Recorder at far left, swearing in the new City Council members on January 5, 1981. Left to right: Dick Benzkofer, Mayor Robert Enright, Alderman at Large Tom Kough, First Ward Alderman Peter Grover, First Ward Alderman Don Sorenson, Second Ward Alderman Donna Robbins, and Third Ward Alderman Bryan Toney.

Approximately 150 people gathered at the Salvation Army on January 5, 1984, to surprise with contributions Johnson and Burzinski, owners of Charley's Bowl and Lounge and Stephen's Supper Club that burned on December 26, 1983.

Lt. Rhona Evenson helping Specialist Timothy Wesly put on a chemical suit during training exercises at the Austin National Guard Armory, April 1991.

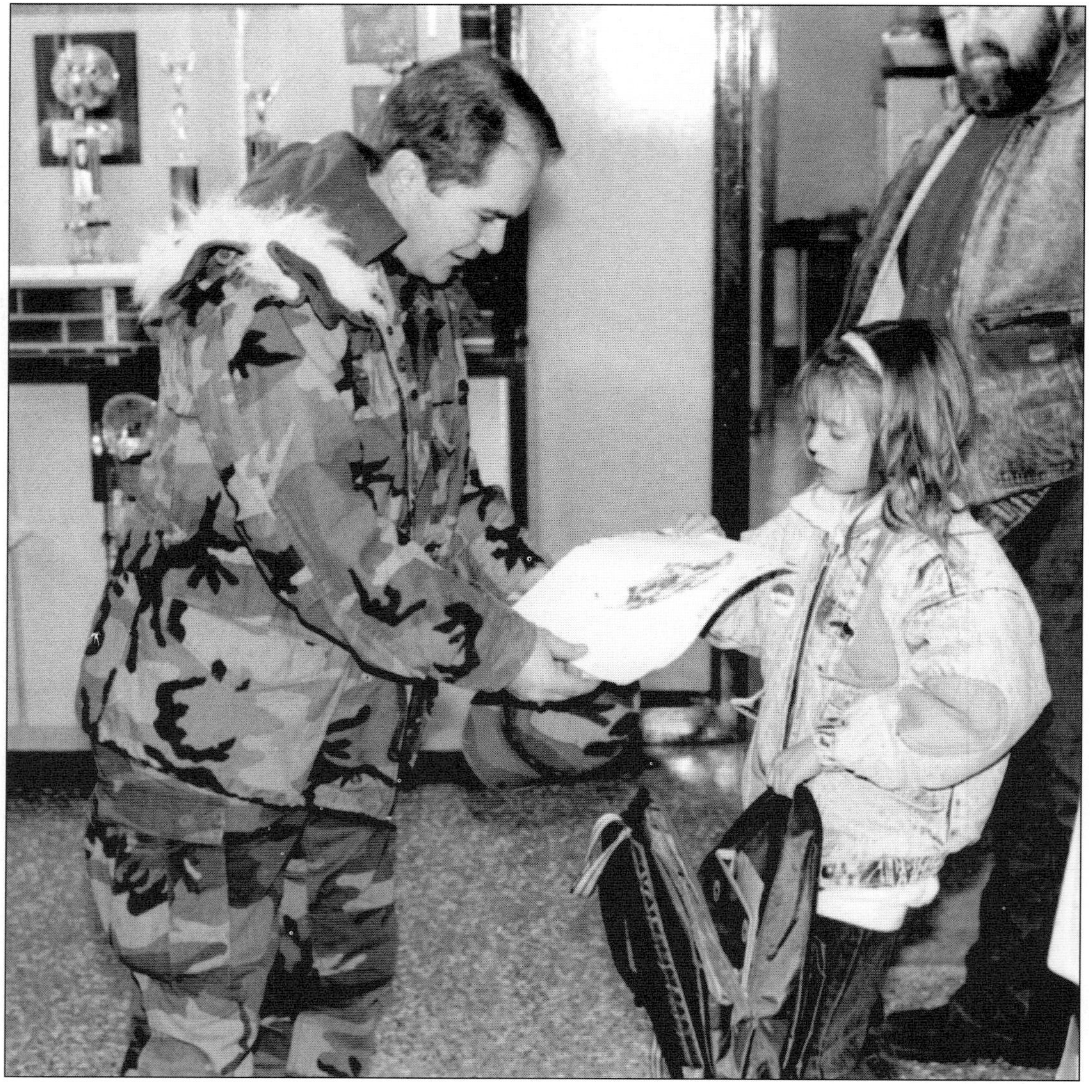

A supporter giving artwork to Bob Kvam at the Austin Armory in December 1990 before he left for Operation Desert Shield.

Public Service ❖ 33

Members of V.F.W. Post 1216 and the Austin High School Marching Band in Austin's traditional Memorial Day parade marching down 1st Avenue NE in 1992.

Television character Alf and Rodney Friedrich, a nationally certified motorcycle instructor, June 1992.

Thousands of tires were unloaded at the Mower County Fairground for the Mower County Recycling Program in April 1991. It was estimated that 24 semi-loads were turned over to the program.

Think Nguyen telling Vietnamese stories to Loc Nguyen, Chris Grove, and Stacy Clingman during "I Love to Read" activities at Oak Park Mall on February 10, 1991.

Starting the cement floor in the senior center, April 1991.

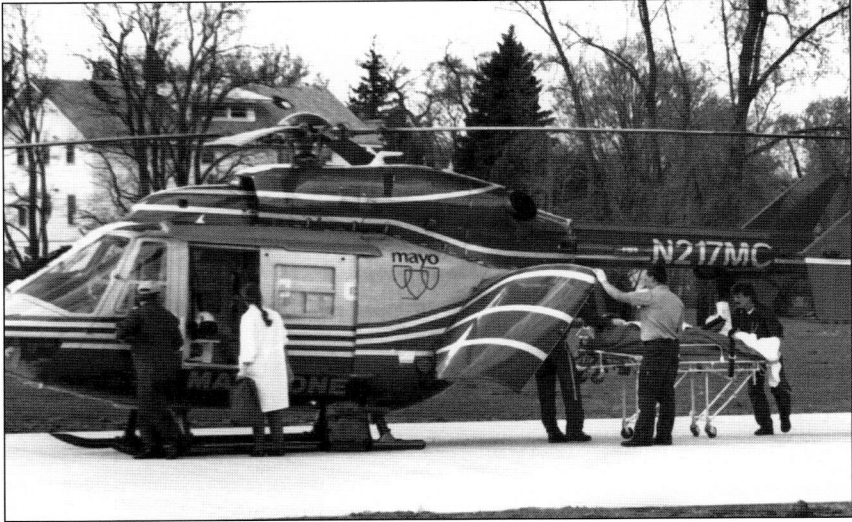
Helicopter Mayo I landing at the Austin Medical Center.

Mike Downey of the American Legion Color Guard and Bud Campbell representing the V.F.W. take part in a flag raising ceremony in front of the Mower County Courthouse, June 1992. The Austin Elks Club sponsored the ceremony in honor of Flag Day. It was also the 100th anniversary of the "Pledge of Allegiance."

John O'Rourke, Austin Mayor from 1987 until 1997.

Barry Simonson became Mower County Sheriff in 1995.

Mayor Bonnie Rietz addressing a packed city council chamber on January 19, 2001. From left to right: Councilman Pete Christopherson and Councilwoman Jeanne Poppe listen as Rietz speaks to members of the audience, including Utilities Director Jerry McCarthy and former Utility Board President Ruth Rasmussen.

Sports raffle for the Red Cross, December 2000. Left to right: Gary Ray, Bonnie Rietz, Amy Klein (Ankeny's), and Captain Curt Rude.

Austin Mayor Bonnie Rietz presents a key to the city to Governor Jesse Ventura prior to his budget speech in Austin at the Hormel Sales cabin January 26, 2001.

Public Service ❖ 37

Auctioneers Dave Thompson and Larry Bunkers volunteered their time at an auction to benefit the Humane Society on Main Street, June 3, 2001.

Cleaning up the graffiti on the sides of buildings, like in the alleyway shown here behind the Culligan building on 2nd Street NE, September 2001. Left to right: George Thomas from the Welcome Center, Mark Bjorlie from the Y.M.C.A., Captain Curt Rude from the Austin Police Department, Howie Strey of Teen Court, and Tony Alonso from Hormel.

Kicking off the fall season for "Spruce Up Austin," September 2001, from left to right: Mike Ruzek; Mayor Rietz; Gretchen Ramlo; Gary Ray, Executive Vice President of Refrigerated Foods of Hormel; and Julie Craven. They are preparing to spread mulch around the 1,000 trees that had been planted during the previous three years.

Austin Public Library at 323 4th Avenue NE, 2002.

The Austin Fire Department's new fire truck, 2002.

Construction along 8th Street NW brought traffic down to two lanes and detoured traffic around projects in August 2002.

Two houses were moved down Mower County 19 by Dave and Dee Whalen for the Austin Municipal Airport runway expansion in August 2002. They were moved to a development at Rose Creek.

Industry

Industry in Austin is marked by Hormel Foods. The symbol of the community for more than 100 years, Hormel continues to play a large role in the development of Austin.

In recent years Hormel has expanded its corporate presence in Austin with the construction of its Corporate South offices on North Main and the opening of the SPAM Museum.

The continuing success of Hormel has also helped the development of corollary industries in Austin. A pallet maker, box makers and others have found success in the community because of ties to Hormel.

Austin Utilities plant, circa 1967.

In front of a Hormel display are, left to right: unknown; Vern Schwaegerle, American Meat Institute; and R. F. Gray of Hormel, circa 1969.

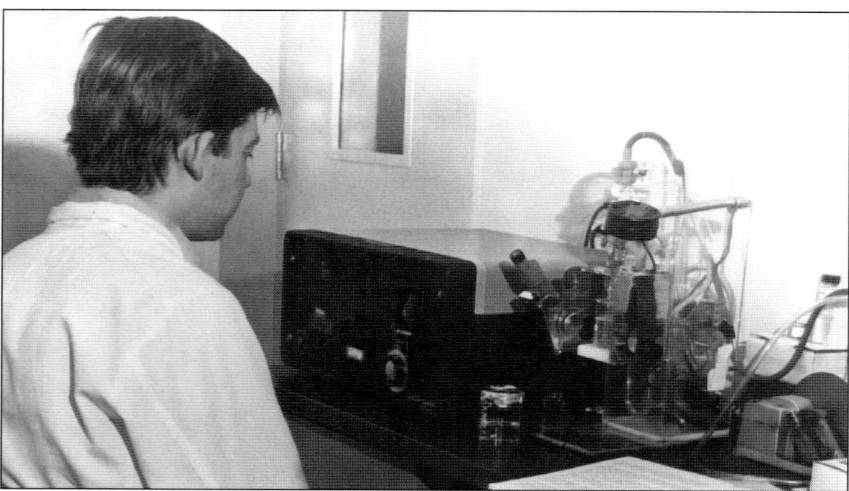

A researcher at the Hormel Institute, circa 1969.

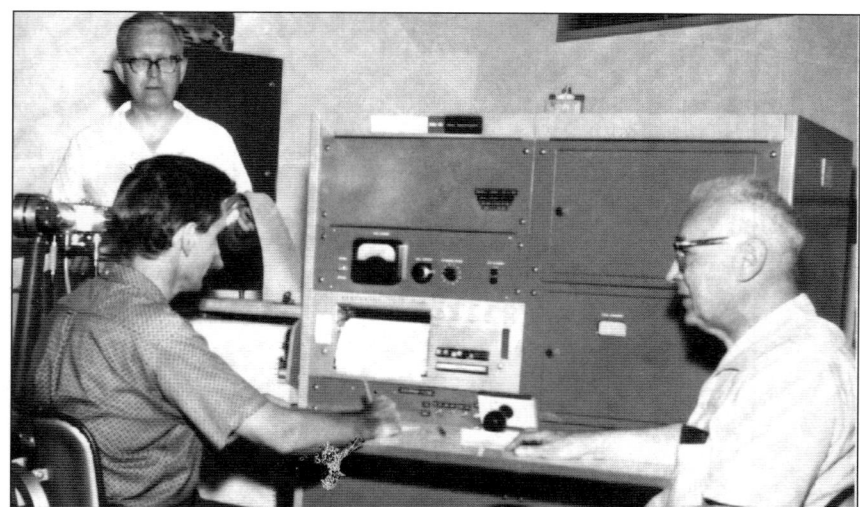

Dr. Ralph Holman, right, at the Hormel Institute, 1965. He started at the Hormel Institute in 1951 working on research in fatty acids. He previously taught at the University of Minnesota Medical School.

Industry ❖ 41

Hormel Institute, circa 1965. Ground was broken for the $600,000 building in 1959, and the Institute moved into the new building in 1960.

A temporary addition was built adjoining the Microbiology Section of the Hormel Institute in 1968.

Dr. Shigery Makino and Dr. Toshino Fukazawa, researchers at the Hormel Institute, July 1969. Makino worked on the lipid analysis of micro-organisms and Fukazawa studied lipid metabolism in liver.

Tze-Ken Yang and Samuel Yu, researchers at the Hormel Institute, July 1969. Yang worked on biochemical indices of stress present in blood and Yu worked with the metabolism of organisms.

Joseph Construction Co. building apartments at 14th Avenue NW in 1969.

Clearing the area for an addition to the Hormel Institute in December 1963.

Hormel Experimental Farm, June 1969.

Ralph Day, owner of Austin Products Inc. at 104 11th Street NE, operating a vinyl laminator he constructed, 1971.

Beginning construction of the Austin Utilities warehouse across the street from the Municipal Building in October 1976.

Hormel Research and Development building, 1975.

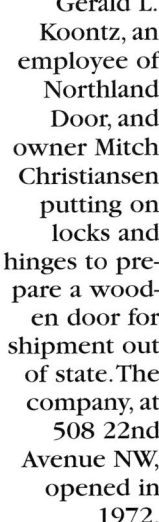

Gerald L. Koontz, an employee of Northland Door, and owner Mitch Christiansen putting on locks and hinges to prepare a wooden door for shipment out of state. The company, at 508 22nd Avenue NW, opened in 1972.

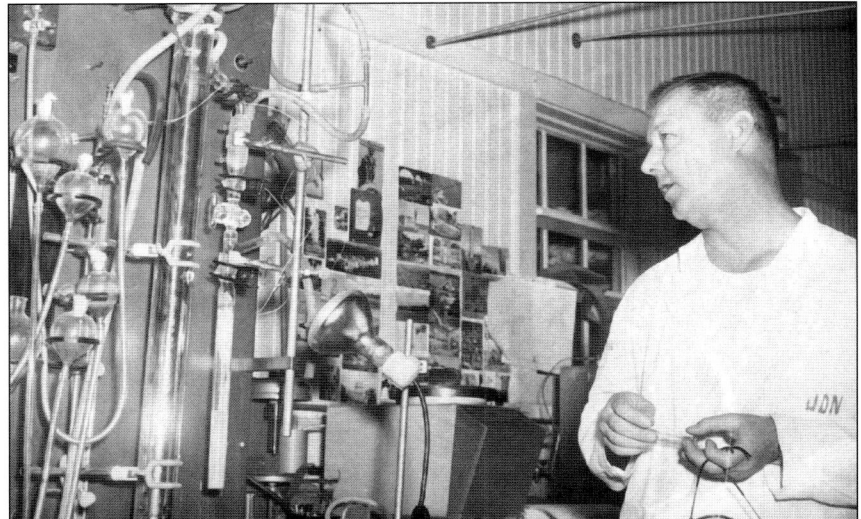

Jon Nadenicek in the Hormel Institute, circa 1979.

A piece of wastewater equipment distributed by the Environmental Equipment Corporation to three members of N.K.M. Industries of Tokyo, Japan, March 1979. Left to right: T. Kaamata, H. Chyou, owner Chris Theissen, and F. Mitomi. Chyou and Mitomi purchased the manufacturing and distribution rights for Japan for E.E.C. equipment.

Industrial Development Corporation of Austin officers for 1978. Left to right: Tom Koeck, secretary-treasurer; Loren Capretz, vice-president; and Don Austin, president.

Oliver Lawrence and Pat Bandi examining lab animals in the Hormel Institute in 1974.

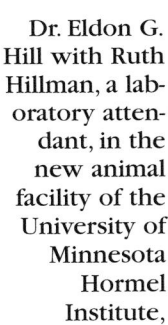

Dr. Eldon G. Hill with Ruth Hillman, a laboratory attendant, in the new animal facility of the University of Minnesota Hormel Institute, 1982.

The Shipping Department at the Austin Hormel plant where boxed products were readied for loading into trucks, circa 1982.

Building the new Hormel plant in 1980.

Groundbreaking ceremonies for Northwest By-Products on February 10, 1982. Left to right: Northwest President Bernie Hurley, Alderman Louie Anthonisen, Mayor Robert Enright, Alderman Peter Grover, Chuck Wilson, Ken Strom, Phil Nolan, and Loren Capretz.

Industry ❖ 47

President of Hormel R. L. Knowlton with a group during the celebration of Hormel's 100th anniversary, 1991. George A. Hormel started the company in 1891 in an abandoned creamery on the banks of the Red Cedar River in Austin. Within three years, a large two-story brick building was going up behind the creamery, the first of a number of expansions at the site.

Hormel Foods on North Main Street, 2002.

Weyerhaeuser's Austin plant superintendent Sterling Brody speaks to second shift workers during a dinner in celebration of earning the Minnesota Safety Council's Governor's Saftey Award, April 4, 2002.

Jon Boyer, Rey Veraza, Jeremy Pedersen, and Tim Camerer of Precision Signs pose amidst some of the components of the giant new Paramount Theatre marquee, June 15, 2002.

Schools & Churches

Providing a quality education for children has been important to all those who have called Austin home. From its early days and continuing through today, Austin's education system is a rallying point for the community.

Austin continues to meet the challenge of educating today's children. In recent years many of the buildings have been modernized to accommodate today's high-tech learning and athletic facilities are being improved to insure Austin's athletes have the best training and experience.

All of the changes and improvements to the educational facilities in Austin have been done while maintaining a connection to the community's rich history. School buildings and athletic fields have been remodeled, instead of replaced, offering students and athletes a reminder of their roots.

Pacelli High School graduates receiving their diplomas in June 1969.

Schools & Churches ❖ 49

Austin Area Vocational Technical graduates receiving their diplomas in 1969.

Students receiving their diplomas during Austin Junior College commencement from President R.I. Meland in June 1969.

Austin High School graduates receiving their diplomas in June 1969.

Pacelli graduation, 1966.

Pacelli High School students marching in downtown Austin during a homecoming parade in 1969.

Schools & Churches ❖ 51

Pacelli High School students prepare for their 1967 Homecoming.

Reverend Earle Tousley and Stephen Price participating in the groundbreaking for Bethlehem Free Methodist Church in August 1967.

Austin High School class of 1932 celebrate their 45th reunion in 1977. Front row, left to right: Esther Kirchner, Dorothy Kirchner Kolberg, Viola Gordon Hall, Thelma Wandas Anderson, and Ervin Peterson. Back row: Rita Mahacek Seeger, Evelyn Low Fellows, Howard Hall, Elizabeth Nelson DeMoses, and Elsie Hemmingsen Culton.

Austin High School's class of 1932 held its 45th reunion in 1977. Front row, left to right: Atlanta Bell Fiksdal, Margaret Johnson, Lois Braun Diercks, Edith Heimsness Dugan, and Gladys Buringa Peterson. Included in back row: Kenneth Garbich, Edna Kearns Morgan, and Richard Morgan.

Austin High School class of 1932 celebrate their 45th reunion in 1977. Back row, left to right: Lucille Brooks Bates, Mary Luksik Shulty, Bea Furtney Sheedy, Mildred Ulwelling Anderson, and James Anderson. Front row: Ferris Furtney, Frances Erickson Granholm, Allen Oxley, Florence Vogel, and Winslow Casey.

Austin High School class of 1932 celebrates their 45th reunion in 1977. Pictured are: Helen French Sorenson, Marion Copley Stern, Harriet Snell McAnnany, Ruth Rierson Gullickson, and Elizabeth Schwam Gerhart. Back row: Walton Johnson, Lilah Peterson Ludvigson, Charles Stern, Margaret Ames Peach, and Frank Erdman.

Groundbreaking ceremonies for Faith Evangelical Lutheran Church on 4th Drive SW near 21st Avenue SW on May 10, 1982. Left to right: Pastor Matthew Majovski; Dean Pacholl, President of Faith Building Committee; Earl Bruckmeier, building committee co-chairman; building committee members Jerry Henricks, Leion Jacobson, John Tomhave; David Kane, architect; Dale Beckel, representing general contractor Joseph Construction Company; and Terry Fox, Fox Electric.

Pacelli High School at 311 4th Street NW in 1982. St. Augustine Catholic Church is in on the right.

Pacelli High School in June 1980.

Austin High School class of 1932 gathered for their 50th reunion in 1982. Back row, left to right: Walden Johnson, Howard Hall, and Ferris Furtney. Included in the front row: Marguerite Peterson Furtney, Viola Gordon Hall, and Elsie Hemmingsen Culton.

Pacelli High Golden Scroll winners, 1982. Left to right: Michael Hansel, Susan Bissen, Scott Peterson, and sponsor Ronald Herzog.

Dr. Richard Morrison became the Austin school district superintendent in February 1981.

Out-of-state classmates from Austin High School's class of 1932 celebrated their 50th reunion in 1982.

Austin High School class of 1934 gathered in 1984 for their 50th reunion. Front row, left to right: Stan Stephenson, Grace Gleason Dooley, June Puchta Morgan, Ione Barnitz Bell, Edith Hartson Pike, Mary Marmesh Radl, Irene Schroeder Tapp, Harold Burroughs, Evelyn Daily DuMond, Orphis Barsgard Grap, Gertrude Bungum Behndt, Joe Vorhees, Clara Underland Chilson, Evelyn Redwing Christopherson, Maxine Sherrer Howe, Norma Howells Tyrer, Bernice Apold McNally, and Helen Hallman Swingen. Second row: Norman Stuewer, Gwendolyn Low Earl, Arlene Lesch Bjork, Gladys Jarvis Lillie, Rachel Weseman Neiswanger, Marion Welken, Frances Jenson Laufle, Florence Konovsky Hogan, Mildred Booher Becker, Lorna Stempson Parnell, Leona Padelford Kehret, Genieve Cressey, Gladys Johnson Mechenich, and Edna Wood Freeland. Third row: Margeruite Stephens Earl, Kathleen Holdren Wilson, Helen Larson Hull, Sullivan, Marcella Block, Harriet Earl Ryan, Marjorie Wilson Wilson, Margeruite Fischer Esse, Frances Felch Morse, Mildred Bertilson Clawson, Thelma Brandt Birmingham, Bernice Ward Staples, Margaret Rossow Heuton, Ruth Braun Garner, Dorothy Dugan Lade, Kermit Olson, and Shirley Pethrn Carlson. Fourth row: Claude Bump, Dick Warrington, John Lafferty, James Sathre, Floyd Viall, Joseph "Percy" Mitchell, Cecil Misgen, Jerry Maloney, Nelson Earl, and Lyall Larson.

Austin Community College at 1600 8th Avenue NW. It became Riverland Community College in 1996 when it was merged with the technical college. It has facilities in Austin, Albert Lea, and Owatonna.

Austin Technical Institute at 1900 8th Avenue NW. It merged with the community college in 1996.

Pacelli High School students performed a female version of Neil Simon's "The Odd Couple" in April 1991 in the Queen of Angels Theatre. In rehearsal, left to right: Cara Cotter, Camille Bohrer, Megan Gale, and Sarah Pfeil.

Fifth through eighth graders competed for the spelling district title on February 12, 1992. Left to right: Matt Mullenback, eighth grade second place; Mandy Dress, eighth grade champion to advance to the Regional Bee; and Becky Miller, sixth grade third place.

Stacey Klaehn putting a newspaper article on the board in her fourth grade classroom at Southgate Elementary. Teacher Shari Allen had students use the *Austin Daily Herald* as a learning tool every Tuesday and Thursday. February 1991.

Neveln Elementary School fifth graders examining an earth ball while learning about Earth Day at the J.C. Hormel Nature Center, April 1992.

St. Olaf Lutheran Church's Wee Learning Center children presenting aluminum tabs to McDonald's as a part of a fund-raising effort to defray expenses of families staying at the Ronald McDonald House in Rochester, April 1991.

Students of Lisa Deyo's third and fourth grade combination class painting a flag on the windows of their Shaw School room, 1991. Left to right: Angie Uher, Chelsea Anderson, Theresa Sanchez, and Jessica Corkill.

Schools & Churches ❖ 59

Banfield elementary students raised $2,472.75 in the Jump Rope for Heart contest, April 1991. Top row, left to right: Brook Zabel, Peter Russell, Kyle Sinz, and physical education teacher Donna Judson. Middle row: Ryonne Underhill, Amie Burton, Julie Gillis, and Mandy Flack. Front row: Dannielle Berg, Melissa Dickhut, Chelsea McColley, Jason Baskin, and Jami Iverson.

An addition being built at Banfield Elementary School in April 1992.

The Austin High School Future Farmers of America observed National F.F.A. month in February 1991. Front row, left to right: Tom Clennon, John Carroll, Mark Severtson, Jon Hllier, Tina Strouf, and Naida Mattice. Second row: Tom Wicks, Shannon Becker, Terry Magnuson, and Jon Jovaag. Third row: Robert Schmidt, Julie Smith, Rita Becker, Kay Heers, and Debbie Murphy. Back row: Jason Schlichter, Frank Peterson, and Paul Martell.

First graders in Sandy Shile's class at Neveln School gathered around their Christmas tree offering their reasons for the season in 1990.

Telstar 4-H club purchased school supplies for students in the English As A Second Language Program at Austin High School in February 1992.

The first team to finish the crab race and build a pyramid were declared the winners when over 100 sixth through ninth graders gathered at the Ellis Middle School for Thursday Night Thunder, sponsored by Innovative Outreaches United Inc. of Austin, March 1991.

Schools & Churches ❖ 61

Justin Enfield, a Queen of Angels third grader, demonstrating how his project on energy conservation works at the fifth annual Austin Science Fair at the Oak Park Mall in February 1991.

Lillian Welch, a resident of St. Mark's Lutheran Home, reading with Phetnarong Phomsoukja, a second grader at Southgate School, during a weekly reading session that paired seniors with students, April 1991.

Matt Holden with his police dog at an Austin school.

Crash Test Dummies Vince and Larry shook hands at the D.A.R.E. chemical free family picnic for D.A.R.E. graduates at the Austin swimming pool, June 1992.

Firefighter Ron Felten read a story and demonstrated his gear to Teresa Royce's second grade class at Queen of Angels School in February 1991.

Faith Lutheran Church at 2103 8th Street SW, circa 1991.

Cedar River Church of Christ at 1006 12th Street SW, 1991.

Schools & Churches ❖ 63

Austin High School's graduating class of 1990.

Faith Evangelical Free Church at 1805 12th Street SW, April 1999.

Westminster Presbyterian Church at 801 6th Street SW, May 1999.

St. Paul's Lutheran Church at 2100 16th Street SW, May 1999.

Bethlehem Free Methodist Church at 1500 4th Avenue SE, June 1999.

Crane Community Chapel at 1111 9th Street NE, April 1999.

Kingdom Hall of Jehovah's Witnesses at 2115 5th Avenue SE, June 1999.

New Life Vineyard Christian Fellowship at 210 4th Street NE, 1999.

First Congregational Church at 1910 3rd Avenue NW, April 1999.

A new cross is placed atop St. Augustine Church, 196 feet from the ground, August 2002. Made of copper and a gold leafed finish, the hollow 26-pound cross, with a lightning rod on top, replaced the cross damaged in a 1976 lightning strike.

Ellis Middle School choir director Jeff Schei leads a group of eight graders in practicing songs for their upcoming Christmas concert, December 2000.

Worshippers at St. Olafs Lutheran Church in Austin light candles for a procession in memory of AIDS victims December 3, 2000.

Sumner Elementary School Librarian Jan Thomas reads Dr. Seuss "Horton Hatches the Egg" to children at the Austin Public Library in observance of the author's birthday and Read Across America week, March 4, 2001.

Sumner Elementary School fifth grader Cory Vielhauer, left, won the fourth and fifth grade geography bee January 5, 2001, while friend and classmate Tim Harber took second place.

Schools & Churches ❖ 67

Austin High School D.E.C.A. students from left, Lyndsey DeVries, Trina Fisher, Dan Smith, and Michael Hansen were on their way to Anaheim, California, after winning first place in the state competition, March 2001.

On May 10, 2001, the previous year's teacher of the year Katie Ulwelling passed the torch to the 2001 winner, Margo Bissen, a kindergarten through fifth grade music teacher at Sumner Elementary.

Banfield Elementary School third graders in Marcia Wilson's and Dale Rogers's class visited the historic Excelsior School House at the Mower County Fairgrounds, May 17, 2002.

The red bricks of St. Augustine Catholic Church were repaired on a northeast belltower, May 2002.

Aaron Rieker, right, pauses while standing outside St. Augustine's Church awaiting Pacelli High School graduation ceremonies, June 7, 2002.

Sports & Leisure

Start talking Austin athletics and you're bound to get a pretty stern and proud response. The community takes great pride in the accomplishment of its local high school athletic teams as well as its many amateur teams.

Perhaps best known for its amateur baseball in the 1940s and 1950s, Austin continued to produce its share of winners and great athletes during the 1970s, 1980s and 1990s.

Austin High's football team remained strong while upstart programs like boys and girls hockey and girls basketball left their respective marks in the history books. Not to be outdone Pacelli High fielded its share of Cinderella stories as well, including a memorable boys state basketball championship in the 1990s.

The Packers, sponsored by First Bank of Austin, placed second in the eleventh and twelfth grade girls' division at the Timberwolves Hoop Festival. From left to right: Teri Watkins, Kelly Haukom, Jenna Nerby, and Theresa Lang.

Dave Bonella inside the pro shop of the Austin Country Club, 1966.

The pro shop at the Austin Country Club shortly after opening in November 1967.

Austin Symphony and Chorus in November 1965.

Sports & Leisure ❖ 71

Waiting to tee off at an Austin golf course.

Golfers Lillian Flynn (2nd low gross), Julianne Bawek (1st low gross), Gloria Weis (2nd low gross), and Judy McGuire (1st low net).

An Austin V.F.W. baseball game.

East Side Lake fishing pier.

Harley Ladlu, 95 years old, and Alice Johnson, 91, at the bowling alley.

Skybox demo derby at the 1985 Mower County Fair.

Bubbles the Clown, Mark Goty, handing out balloon animals to the kids.

Childrens archery competition at the Mower County Fair in 1985.

Serving refreshments at the Mower County Fair in 1985.

Sports & Leisure ❖ 73

Swimming in the pool at the Y.M.C.A., circa 1981.

Relaxing in the hot tub at the Y.M.C.A., circa 1981.

Ages 10 and under swimming class, circa 1989. Front row, left to right: Cimarron Anderson, Ryan Picker, Peter Jones, Thor Johnson, Kyle Gulbrandson, John Maus, and Rachel Leger. Back row: Susan Weldon, Crystal Budahn, Heidi Bremner, Megan Loeschen, Erica Ash, Hilary Johnson, Kristi Foster, and April Leger.

On a ride during a Rose Creek anniversary celebration in June 1991 are, left to right: Lindsey Lukes, age 4, Sherri Baumbach, and Brittany Helmer, age 2.

Todd Park complex in 1983.

Austin High School Rhythmics Danceline during halftime of the Austin-Faribault boys basketball game, January 11, 1990.

The Austin Community College golf team successfully defended its state title, 1992. Left to right: coach Phil Bundy, Mark Severson, Cory Renchin, Tim Haldorson, Ryan Brandt, and Kirk Peterson.

Pacelli 1990-91 girls basketball team. Front row, left to right: Jenny Fryer, Laura Van Hyfte, Cara Cotter, and Tammie Treuter. Back row: Renee Bellrichard, Lori Dawes, Sandy Schottler, Lisa Quednow, and Camille Bohrer.

Shane King trying his luck at ax throwing, 1991.

Andy LeVasseur at his home at 1001 18th Street practicing his golf swing, March 1991.

Bowling award winners in the Saturday Prep Division, April 1992. Front row, left to right: Darcy Edge, Tyler Esse, and Melissa Placek. Second row: Aaron Bellrichard, Brandon Fette, Chad Javay, and Amanda Young.

Bowling award winners in the Saturday Juniors/Majors Division, April 1992. Front row, left to right: Scott Sayles, Brian Butts, David Morse, Josh Kowbow, Tony Edge, and Jason Weber. Second row: Katie Deters, Nikki Kroneman, Julie Sayles, Sheila Hanegraaf, and Jim Juenger. Third row: Jamie Brandt, Chad Carlson, Tim Kroneman, Scott Wildeman, and Derek Placek.

The seventh grade girls traveling basketball team finished their 1991 season 28-5. Front row, left to right: Jenna Nerby, Gina Berthiaume, Kiesha Wetterberg, Julie Kvam, Julie Mitties, and Kelly Logterman. Back row: coach Jim Berthiaume, Jenny Beckel, Jenny Blaser, Katie Raso, Angie Andt, coach Randy Kvam, and coach Dan Blaser.

Pacelli 1990-91 boys basketball team. Front row, left to right: Pete Leuer, Rob Garry, Aaron Johnson, Steve Rogne, and Matt Johnson. Back row: Marty Wolesky, Chris Loescher, Jake Nelson, Ricky Njos, Jason Mandler, and Jon Johnson.

Mike and Matt Kuiper and Andy Mitlyng crossing Dobbins Creek at the Hormel Nature Center, April 1992.

Pacelli High School plays Lake City High School in volleyball on September 12, 1991. Players, left to right: Michelle Purcell, Laura Backel, and Laura Van Hyfte.

Austin High School 1990-91 wrestling team. Front row, left to right: Josh Knox, Alex Rayman, Derek Johnson, John Bergstrom, and Tracy Smith. Middle row: Nate Ollman, Dave Bednar, John Carroll, Brian Lammey, Sean Donaghue, Jess Dunlap, and Zach Ollman. Back row: Mike Minnick, Toby Schommer, Brian Schultz, Matt Callahan, Sam Amdahl, and Todd Bina.

Pacelli 1990-91 wrestling team. Front row, left to right: Scott Brophy, Justin Miller, John Weis, and Justin Bushaw. Back row: Dave Coyle, Troy Miller, Shannon Wilde, Eric Baldus, and Jayson Pettiford.

Cross Country runners at the Austin Invite on October 3, 1991. The Pacelli runner is Jeff Tilkes; Austin runner is Noel Karl.

Youth bowling league award winners, June 1991. Front row, left to right: Katie Deters, Michelle Jensen, Bryce Wells, Amanda Young, Darcy Edge, and Mark Lang. Second row: Janelle Young, Mikayle Klinger, Julie Sayles, Steph Holets, Tricia Culbert, Mandi Norregaard, and Gretchen Schumacher. Third row: John Holvorson, Paul Bellrichard, Randy Augustine, Nate Schrom, Tom May, Keri Haney, and Nikkie Kroneman.

Dan Burke running the football for Knights of Columbus team in September 1991.

Cara Cotter of Pacelli High School spinning to the left to open herself to the hoop in a February 1992 game with Kasson-Mantorville.

Austin High School girls basketball players wearing their championship medals in July 1991.

Queen of Angels 1993-94 seventh grade girls basketball team. Front row, left to right: Brigette Bedner, Katie Ulwelling, Amanda Draayer, Melissa Price, Patty Servin, and Jenny Klapperich. Back row: Jackie Byam, Laura Sheedy, Melissa Blaser, Karen Darveaux, Sara Wencl, and Brook Erickson.

Leonard Beck returning a shot during an 18-and-under match in the Junior Club Championships at the Austin Country Club in August 1993. He defeated John Leonard 1-6, 6-4, 6-3.

Austin High School's Jennifer Fox and Rachelle Tveter dive for the ball during their second volley ball game against Faribault on August 29, 1991.

Austin High School's Ryan Bonorden shooting with less than a minute left in the game on February 4, 1992.

Austin girls basketball post game celebration after defeating Northfield in the Region 1AA first round game, February 1991.

Swimmers at the Big 9 meet on October 27, 1990.

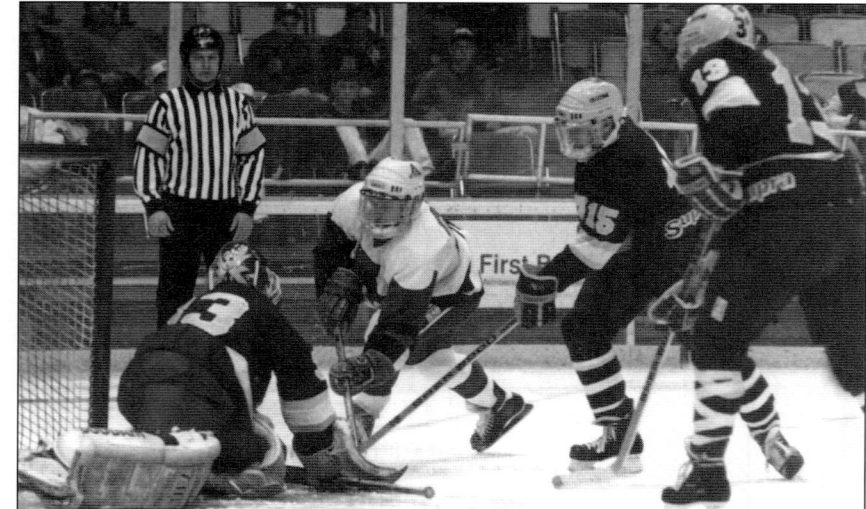

Packer junior Noel Karl rushing in on Apple Valley goaltender Joe Morris during the first period of the consolation semi-final at the St. Paul Civic Center in March 1993. Austin won the game 2-1.

Sports & Leisure ❖ 83

Austin on the field at the Austin-Osseo game in May 1990 at Midway Stadium in St. Paul.

Austin V.F.W.'s John Frein scoring the team's second run on a triple by Ben Kvam, July 1993. Austin beat Faribault.

Austin ball players Bob Peters and Ryan Rassmussen in May 1990.

Austin Packer runner Ryan Bell breaking out of the blocks for the start of the boys spring medley relay during a co-ed track meet against Fairmont at Wescott Field, April 1992.

Austin soccer team of 1990.

Ceder River Days one mile run on July 4, 1991.

Austin 1990-91 boys basketball team. Front row, left to right: Kyle Finney, Jason Schmit, Wade Kubat, Dan Eckmann, and Darren Lewis. Middle row: Jason McClary, Jason Gerhardt, Tim Goetz, Jay Beck, and Jim Davison. Back row: Nathan Finney, Brian Mair, Kevin Mitties, Shawn Dryden, Jason Long, Bob Lenz, and Andrew Elwer.

Austin 1990-91 hockey team. Front row, left to right: Brian Bakker, Ken Ree, Dave Matzko, Jeremy Nord, assistant coach Monte Prieve, Troy Schaefer, head coach Tim Guyer, Todd Gibson, Dave Anderson, and Matt Cano. Middle row: Aaron Kahle, Randy Pepper, Steve Thompson, Noel Karl, Geoff Pepper, Rob Haedt, Tim Peterson, Conrad Ray, Tom Hoffman, and Chad Wolfe. Third row: Steve Bremner, Nate Richardson, Jeremy Olson, Jerod Jacobsen, Mark McMasters, Sam Bergstrom, Steve Nemitz, and manager Jeff Daily.

Austin High School's Ben Dolan sending a Cloquet player flying after a ferocious check during consolation action at the St. Paul Civic Center in March 1993.

Austin sophomore Sara Usgaard backhand returning during a tennis practice in August 1993.

Austin girls basketball player Heidi Rietz shoots during the third period of an Austin-Rochester girls basketball game on February 9, 1992.

Austin 1990-91 girls basketball team. Front row, left to right: Rachelle Tveter, Ann Bartholmey, Heidi Rietz, and Amy Hovland. Back row: Jackie Burke, Jennifer Fox, Darcy Klapperick, Debbie Urick, and Heidi Berthiaume.

Austin's V.F.W. baseball team watches from the dugout.

Pacelli seventh and eighth grade volleyball players on October 29, 1990.

Scott Delaney vs. Chad Olson, circa 1993. Scott became the national champion at the Northern Plains Wrestling Tournament. He took first-place at 115 pounds in the freestyle competition for individuals 14 and under and also took second place in the 115 pound Greco-Roman competition.

Austin High School cross country runner Colleen Larson running in the Austin Invite on October 3, 1991.

Pacelli boys basketball team won the District 2A trophy on March 3, 1991.

Mike Swank of Lyle is thrown out at second by Pacelli's catcher Casey Anderson after Carl Trukenmiller struck out during the Pacelli vs. Lyle District 2A Championship game on May 29, 1991.

Sports & Leisure ❖ 91

Austin Athletic Hall of Famers on February 8, 1991.

Kirk Paulson, Timothy Camerer, Gordy Handeland, and Greg Meyer performed in "The Music Man" at the Austin Community College Theater, February 1992.

Tom Koeck, David Stilwell, Nat Goudy, Emery "Bud" Thompson, James McNally, and Liz Ackerwold-Erickson were inducted into the Austin High School Hall of Fame on February 14, 1992. Pictured, left to right: Tom and Marion Koeck, David and Cheryl Stilwell, James Goudy (Nat's son) and Dorothy (Nat's widow), Dorothy (Thompson's daughter), "Bud" and Enid Thompson, Patsy and James McNally, and Liz and Neal Ackerwold-Erickson.

Austin's Dana Matthews releasing a pitch during the seventh inning, April 1992. She pitched a no hitter with the Packers defeating Albert Lea 8-0 at Todd Park.

Snowmobilers on Austin's East Side Lake took advantage of the newly fallen snow and warm temperatures on February 2, 2002.

Rehearsing for "Ms. Nelson is Missing," put on by the Matchbox Childrens Theatre at the Paramount, February 2002.

Disasters

Austin saw its share of disasters during the 1970s, 1980s and 1990s.

Flooding caused by the Cedar River and Turtle Creek devastated the community in all three decades. Community leaders continue today to search for a flooding solution, but as the events of the three decades demonstrated – a solution has been slow in coming.

Cold weather and big snow falls unsurprisingly swept through all three decades as well. And a strong wind storm in the late 1990s destroyed many of the city's trees.

East Oakland Avenue at its intersection with 4th Street SE was completely under water. The area was one of the first to go under when the Red Cedar River flooded in 1978.

Flooding in March 1965 after the Red Cedar River rose over 5 feet. The river crested at 19.4 feet which set a new record.

Houses after the Cedar River flooded in March 1965. More than 50 homes were evacuated during the flood.

Looking from the stone bridge on 4th Street SE, these homes were evacuated due to the flooding of the Cedar River in March 1965.

Turtle Creek water rose over two feet in March 1965 flooding surrounding areas. Damage to Austin's homes and businesses was over $1 million during the 1965 flood, the worst flooding since 1907.

Disasters ❖ 95

By 10:15 a.m. on December 28, 1966, there was eight inches of snow on the ground with winds at 20 m.p.h.

A fire destroyed Sterling Cleaners and the Sterling Bakery and damaged other stores in the Sterling Shopping Center on July 16, 1973.

Austin Fire Department and Austin Police Department officials at 1708 1st Street NE after an explosion and fire claimed the life of a fourteen year old boy in May 1977. At the far left are firefighter Gary Sherman and Fire Chief Dan Miller.

A resident of 7th Street NE removing snow after six inches of snow fell in 1978.

The Red Cedar River flooded twice in July 1978, the worst floods in Austin's history. On July 7 the river crested at 19 feet three inches. On July 17 it crested at 21 feet nine inches.

Children playing in the street during the flood in 1978. The Austin Fire Department used boats to evacuate residents.

Residents near their homes as the water rapidly rose during a flood in July 1978. Over 200 homes were affected.

Backing into flooded southeast Austin street during a flood in July 1978. No fires or serious traffic mishaps took place during the flood period.

Moving belongings before the flood water seeped into the house in July 1978. During the flood many residents took up residence at the high school where the Red Cross had set up cots.

Residents along 1st Street SE packing and moving their possessions before they could be destroyed by the rapidly rising water July 17, 1978.

Residents moving their belongings after the floods in July 1978. The Red Cross provided cleanup kits and four Red Cross vans toured the flooded areas dispensing food and coffee to flood victims and helping residents.

A victim being carried by Austin firefighters from the Ace Hotel after the hotel caught fire claiming four lives in January 1979.

A fire destroyed a garage at the Phil Dowd residence resulting in an estimated $14,000 loss, June 1982.

Firefighters trying to put out the Ace Hotel fire in January 1979.

Disasters ❖ 99

Turtle Creek with rising waters in March 1982.

Two garages were completely destroyed and a house was damaged in a fire at 711 First Avenue SW in February 1991.

Turtle Creek after it crested at 4.5 feet in 1992.

Labor

Austin is proud of its meat packing heritage. The heritage has resulted in a strong labor movement in the community.

From time-to-time labor and management have not seen eye-to-eye. The largest strike in Austin's history, and one of the bitterest strikes in the history of Minnesota, occurred in Austin in the mid-1980s. Striking meat packers from Local P-9 rallied together and walked out in dispute. The strike reached a pinnacle when the Minnesota National Guard was called in to keep the peace.

Labor peace was eventually restored and the 1990s were the beginning of a calmer period in relations between labor and management in Austin.

Local P-9 supporters during the Hormel strike in 1984.

Hundreds of Austin area dairy farmers dumped over 100,000 pounds of milk during the National Farmers Organization led protest of the low milk prices in March 1967.

Austin teachers picketed the School District Administration building in 1979 to draw attention to the lack of a settlement of a two year contract.

Members of Local 6-578 of the Oil and Chemical Workers Union picketed at Penny's Super Market at 1305 1st Avenue SW on August 28, 1980. The five-day strike ended after a new contract agreement was reached.

Members of Local 6-578 of the Oil and Chemical Workers picketed at Gordy's Super Valu at 905 North Main Street on August 28, 1980. The strike at two supermarkets affected around 80 union members.

Picketers in 1981.

Local P-9 supporters marching in downtown Austin during the Hormel strike in 1985.

A striker speaking at the Hormel strike in 1985.

Local P-9 supporters at a rally during the strike against Hormel in 1985.

During the Hormel P-9 strike in 1985-86, Reverend Jesse Jackson spoke at a rally to support local P-9 and their supporters.

Dan David and Denise Rennells, both Human Service Technicians, stand at the picket lines along 12th Street SW as Minnesota state employees went on strike early on October 1, 2001. The employees, members of the American Federation of State, County, and Municipal Employees, wanted better health care benefits.

A man speaking at a rally to support local P-9 during the Hormel P-9 strike in 1985.

Community

The decades of the 1970s, 1980s and 1990s have brought many changes to the Austin community. A constant has been the community's family atmosphere.

During the years the names, faces and ethnic origins may have changed, but the basic commitment to family has been maintained. With more than 28 community parks and numerous celebrations throughout the year, Austinites enjoy being together.

Whether it's a picnic, or a theatrical or musical performance, or a volunteer event, Austinites continued the practice started by the earliest settlers of giving back to the place they call home.

The following photos show young and old participating in activities that truly make Austin a community.

The ninth annual Farm to Market Day sponsored by the Austin Chamber of Commerce in 1969.

An Austin youngster enjoying winter, circa 1967.

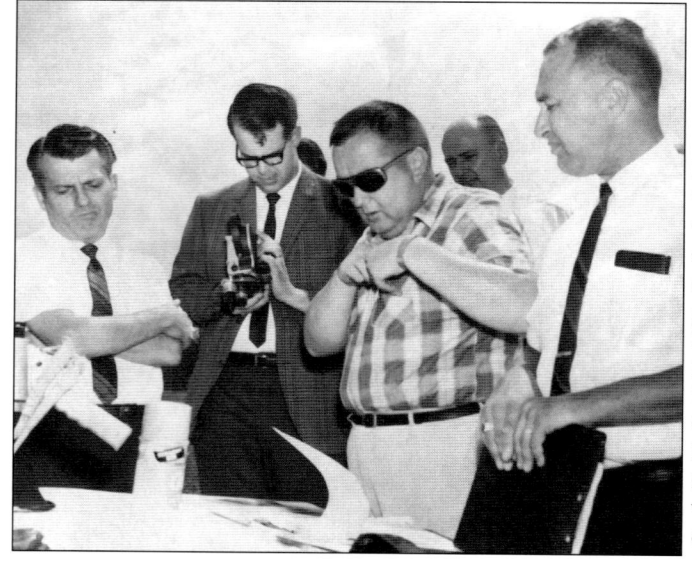
Members of the Austin Chamber of Commerce making final plans for the State Plowing Matches, July 1968. Chamber Manager David McNeil is wearing the dark glasses.

Merril Rolfson receiving an award at a Kiwanis Club meeting in April 1968. Left to right: Robert Sabban, Merril Rolfson, Ben Sanford, and Orin Bowlby.

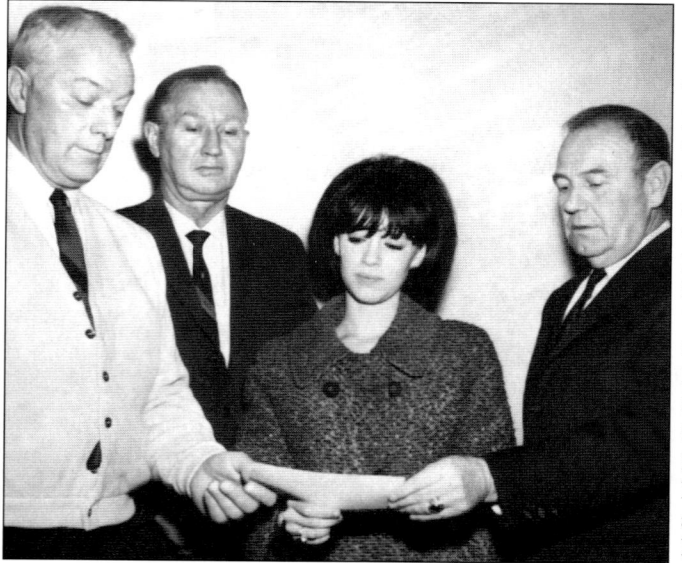
The Austin-Mower County Safety Council presented $5 Courteous Driver awards in January 1969. Left to right: Kenneth Simonsin, Carmen Halstenson, Bonnie Nicol, and Thomas Koeck.

Lancer Daryl VanderHaar and Kidet Scott Anderson with their first place trophy in June 1966.

Jaycee officers for the 1969-70 year. Front row, left to right: Duane Johnson, vice president; Joe Cook, president; and Dr. Norbert Schmitt, out-going president. Back row: James Tweet, director; Richard Benzkofer, treasurer; Hugh Plunkett III, director; David Harbor, director; Dan Greenameyer, state director; and Larry Wilson, secretary.

4-H member Lana Weseman had the champion Southdown wether at the Minnesota State Fair in 1966.

4-H member David Miller was named third place sheep showman at the Minnesota State Fair in 1966.

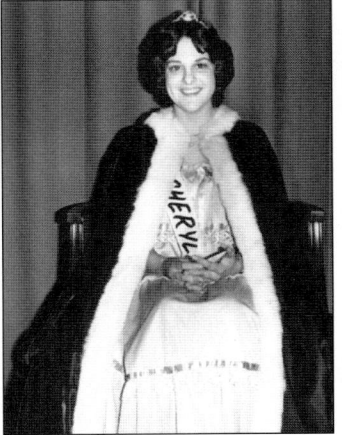

Cheryl Schaefer, a senior at Southland High School, was crowned Mower County Dairy Princess in April 1979.

Mark Husemoller won the Junior Showmanship trophy in the 4-H Barrow Show; on the right is Jill Akkemran who won the Senior Showmanship trophy at the Mower County Fair in 1976.

Austin Fine Arts Civic Group in November 1966. Back row, left to right: Secretary Carol Hardenbergh, Second Vice-President Dr. Claussen, President Roger Plunkett, and First Vice-President Kermith Northwick. Front row: Denise Hompe, Maybelle Johnson, and Wilda Tucker.

1967 Miss Austin finalists. Lynda Plunkett was the winner.

1979 Miss Austin pageant participants. Left to right: fourth runner-up Sheri Hilmer, second runner-up Patricia Stilwell, winner Darcy Voss, first runner-up Debbie Goodwin, and third runner-up Sara Sathre.

The Winkels brothers with their cows at the Mower County Fair in 1985.

The Austin Choralaires in concert in the mid-1960s. Included in back row, left to right: Roger Downing, Nathan Johnson, Mark Joy, Don Siverson, John Wall, Warren Wenzel, Jack Rosenberg, Raymond Ondov, Vernon Barry, and James Olswold. Included in middle row: Mrs. Don Siverson, Mrs. Arthur Bustad, Mrs. Alan Kestner, Mrs. Eugene Arens, Mrs. Kenneth Guy, Mrs. Frank Summerside, and Mrs. James Elliot. Front row: Director Frank Summerside, Mrs. Robert Dahl, Ramona Drake, Karen Beeman, Mrs. James Nesse, and Accompanist Delbert Saman.

Chapter CZ of PEO celebrated its 50th anniversary in April 1992. Left to right: President Jean Clasen, Vice-President Jeanne Winslow, Recording Secretary Mary Juber, Corresponding Secretary Ann Odegaard, Chaplain Jeanyne Hegg, Treasurer Sue Jordan, and Guard Robin Swanson.

Red Cross Chapter Chairman Dan Miller presented Mrs. R. Norman Miller with a pin for her 40 years of volunteer service to the Red Cross, August 1979.

Victims of the flood of 1978 gathered at Lafayette Park for a potluck picnic in July 1979. The picnic was sponsored by FACTS (Floodway Action Citizens Task Source) to mark the first anniversary of one of the city's most destructive disasters.

Greg Olson and his brother Kyle looking through stacks of baseball cards at the baseball card show in Oak Park Mall on April 28, 1991.

John Shaw and Justin Enfield comparing the awards they received at the Cub Scout Banquet at St. Augustine St. Edwards School in February 1991.

Rebecca Loven, age three, kissing her dad goodbye at the Austin Armory in December 1990 before he left for Operation Desert Shield.

Awards were given during the Spamland District Cub Scout-Boy Scout Annual Adult Recognition Banquet at the Westminster Church, April 1991. Left to right: Clifford Chapman, Award of Merit; Gerald Sampson, Silver Scout award; and Art Kuchera, Silver Scout award.

Cyclist Mike Wilson and his son Damian Spear-Wilson, age two, enjoying the weather as they ride through downtown Austin, June 1992.

Parade during Cedar River Days in 1991.

The Twisters performing on the mall for Cedar River Days in July 1991.

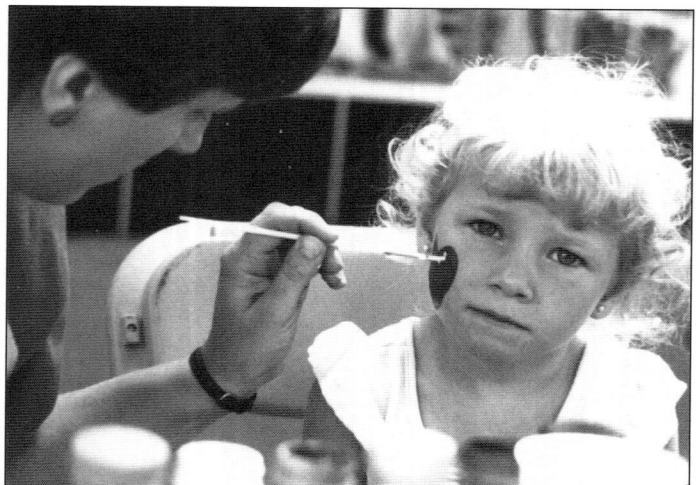
Four year old Ashley Heiny having her face painted by Barb Peterson during Family Days of Cedar River Days, 1991.

Savanah Wheeler and Laurie Hagstrom singing at Cedar River Days in 1991.

Travis Coyle painting a face on his pumpkin during Austin's Labor Force Day in October 1991.

Family Supper in the Plaza Mall for Cedar River Days in 1991.

The Hoe and Grow Club helping make downtown Austin beautiful by planting flowers along Main Street, June 1992. Pictured: Rita Heyer, Muriel Hammer, Marcella Schwartz, Lucille Tolstad, Della Lange, and Della Chinander.

The St. Augustine quilting women making quilts at St. Edwards Elementary School, June 1992. The women had recently given away 50 quilts to migrant workers in the area. Pictured: Eleanor Jennings, Alice Bush, Evelyn Accurso, and Virginia Hartson.

Austin bell ringers performing.

The 1992 Austin Youth Football Board of Directors. Front row, left to right: Bob Wilson, Dennis Maschka, and Walt Hall. Back row: John Ganser, Larry Faber, President Dan Ball, and Dave Ruzek.

Members of the organizing committee of the Symphony Ball's presentation of Fantasia in 1992. Back row, left to right: Jim Heimark, Mark Engelhardt, Marvin Mies, and Marty Fox. Included in second row: Jim Mikkelson, Dr. Richard Nordin, Jerry Lilja, David Hagman, Barbara Hagman, Monnie Rietz, Cathy Moes, and Jim Barber. Front row: Peg Mikkelson, Gloria Nordin, Joan Lilja, Jayna Keimark, Pat Engelhart, Joanne Fox, and Nancy Barber.

1992 Miss Austin and runners-up. Left to right: first runner-up Katherine Hallum, winner Sarah Christiansen, and second runner-up Brenda Radloff.

The Women's Association of Austin Symphony Orchestra met for a luncheon and style show at the First Congregational Church UCC, February 1992. Pictured are, left to right: Jean Nelson, decoration chair; Joanne Fox, coordinator style show; Polly Wells, program chair; Vonnie Snyder, food chair; Nancy Hoversten, president; and Chris Nelson, general chairman.

A banner hung on a light pole during Spam Days.

Spam Singers performing during Spam Days.

Spam Days in 1991.

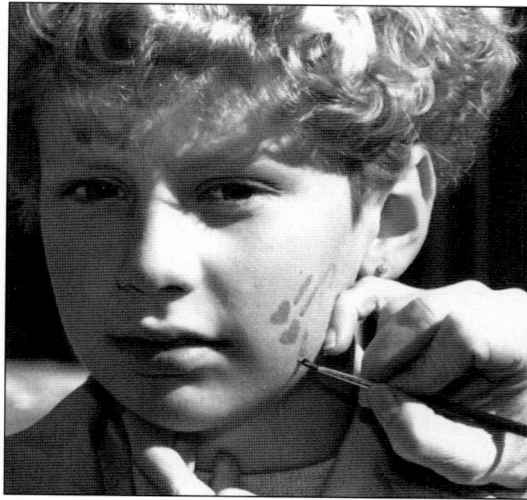
Amy Martin getting her face painted during Austin's Labor Force Day in October 1991.

Dee Wilmot and her granddaughters Michelle and Cherie after tying a yellow ribbon in honor of Dee's son and the children's father, U.S. Army Wayne Wilmot, March 1991.

On March 12, 1991, the anniversary of the founding of the Girl Scouts of America, Brownie Troop No. 7 received its first American flag which was donated by the Austin V.F.W. Post No. 1216.

Curt Srock and son Jeremy, age two, on Father's Day in Todd Park playing on the jungle gym, June 1992.

St. Mark's Lutheran Home celebrated Valentines Day in 1992 by crowning Hermia Thompson and Ray Regner as princess and prince.

Patty Lundberg serves flapjacks with Tim Hoag and Ramsey Johnson at the 41st annual Lions Pancake Day at First United Methodist Church, January 25, 2001.

Jim Percival plows his driveway February 1, 2002, after the area received over six inches of snow the previous day.

Austin High School senior Dan Goettsch steps up to the microphone to ask Brian Sullivan, Minnesota candidate for Governor, a question about the Twins stadium and the contraction issues, February 2002.

A giant pumpkin is taken away after judging at the 2001 Southeastern Minnesota Giant Pumpkin growers weigh-off at Superfresh September 30. Pumpkins ranged in weight from a little over 100 pounds to as heavy at 640 lbs.

Marie Wiese, project chairman for the Keepsake Quilters Guild, poses with Elaine Thon, executive director of the Southern Minnesota Women's Center, and some of the 30 quilts donated by Guild members to the Center for mothers and their babies, March 2001.

Austin Cub Scouts react as Pinewood Derby cars fly by during the Annual Cub Scout Pinewood Derby District Meet February 12, 2001.

Ryan Hill, B.J. Gardner, Chad Enright, and Nick Johnson relaxing under an oak tree behind the outfield fence at Sherman Park, June 1992.

Queen of Angels fifth grader Brandon Holtorf of Austin gets a tip from Less Traff on his game of Snooker at the Mower County Senior Center in Austin, April 2002. Students from the school spent the day at the center learning about different games from Traff.

Our House assisted living center resident Ardeth Olson digs her shovel in the dirt to help plant a new Prairie Fire crab tree at the center in Austin, April 2002. The tree was planted for Arbor Day and was dedicated to the victims of the 9/11 tragedy. "The tree will grow and flourish just as we will as a nation," said Our House Administrator Chris Clements.

Nordean Fox is served her dessert at the Historic Hormel Home in Austin, April 29, 2002. Nearly 100 women gathered for lunch to raise money for the home's new garden.

Fireworks explode over Bandshell Park in Austin July 7, 2002, culminating the Freedom Fest in the Heartland activities.

A crowd of people turned out at the bandshell on Mill Pond for the walk September 19, 2001, including Shirley Magnuson, whose husband has Alzheimer's. Magnuson thanked the participants for their support.

Jack Koppa of Austin walks around the Corcoran Center at St. Edward's Church with his accordion entertaining attendants of the annual Rotary Chicken and Corn Feed, August 4, 2002.

Community ❖ 123

Austin High School freshman Elissa Fisher dances around inside a circle of other attendants of the third annual D.E.D. Special Education Prom held at St. Augustine's Church in Austin, June 2, 2002.

Travis Hammermeister, age eight, of Rose Creek, sweeps up part of a dairy barn as the Mower County Fair began to close down, August 2002.

Packer Arena fundraising leader Larry Lyons, center, accepts a $5,000 check from Deb Bennefeld, vice president of the Riverside Skating Club, August 18, 2002, during a press conference outside the new Austin arena.

Jessica Gerereo, center front, and her two children, Bianca and Emilio, are the new Habitat for Humanity-Freeborn and Mower affiliate homeowning family. From left to right: Mariah Britten, a cousin; Sandra Salinas, a sister; Martha Bronstad, the new owner's mother; and Pam Laskewitz, the family's sponsor. Dedication of the home site at 807 12th Street NE was April 16, 2002.

Gary Grant, left, and Jim Baldus were two of the sponsors of the special prize drawings for the 2001 SPAMTOWN U.S.A. button sales.

Joanne Hansen holds her book "Events I Celebrate" as she sits at her desk in the living room of her home in southeast Austin, June 2002.

North Main Street in Austin's central business district during the Chamber of Commerce's Main Street rummage sales promotion, June 3, 2002. Terry Tracy was among the sellers with his wife Carol and daughter Carrie.

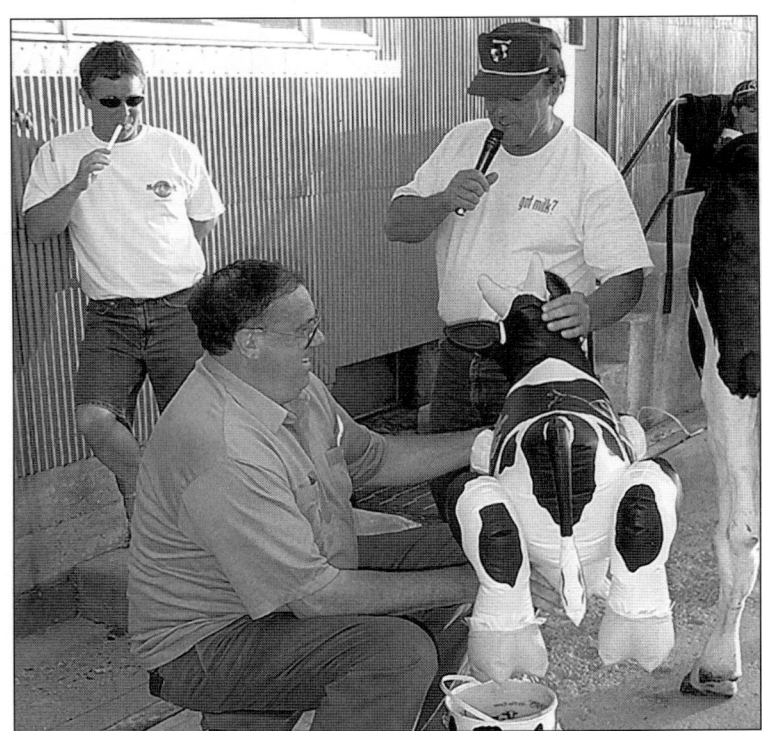

Larry Tompkins, seated, is befuddled by the cow he is told to milk in a Milking Contest by Mower County A.D.A. President Lynn Sathre, with the microphone. Meanwhile, Jim Kiefer, mayor of Taopi, with sunglasses, appears suspicious the contest is rigged. Tompkins, superintendent of Southland Public Schools, won the contest, which ended a weekend of fun at Adams Dairy Days, June 2002.

Pete Heimsness lost his 17-year-old ponytail when co-workers at Weyerhaeuser Paper Company's Austin plant cut it for charity, July 29, 2002. Heimsness, a nine-year employee at the Weyerhaeuser plant, donated the hair to Wigs For Kids, an American Cancer Society program to help children who undergo radiation treatment. Weyerhaeuser corrugated crew second shift employees contributed $270 and the company matched the amount, which went to the Cancer Society.

The SPAMTOWN U.S.A. Festival director Cindy Samuel, board members, and committee chairpersons are surrounded by some of the over 600 boxes of festival trinkets, T-shirts, and other items for distribution at the annual celebration, July 4-8, 2002.

Haley Charnecki and Tristanna Bickford, right, went wading in a sea of pink plastic pigs at the 2001 SPAM Jam celebration at East Side Lake Park, July 8, 2002. In return for grabbing one of the floating porkers, the girls collected prizes.

Shoppers browse one of many vegetable stands at the Farmer's Market, examining this selection of onions, July 2002.

Sophia Rose Smith, a Mower County Dairy Princess attendant, and Mower County A.D.A. members Lynn Sathre and Roger Read distributed half-pints of milk to the crowd watching the 4-H Dairy Show at the Mower County Fair, August 9, 2002.

Seated holding their trophies after a successful Sunday afternoon at the 2002 Mower County Fair Old-time Fiddlers Contest are top winners, left to right: Olaf Hanson, adult division; Jordan Price, novice division; and Joshua Froiland, junior and "high stakes" divisions.

The lunch crowd descended on Herb and Murl's, a Mower County Fair fixture for nearly 30 years, in search of a cool place to eat fair favorites like corn dogs, sno cones and cheese curds, August 2002.

Tina and Lena had the crowd in stitches as they delivered their Scandinavian humor mixed with a variety of songs, August 9, 2002.

Two 450-pound aluminum signs were mounted on the SPAM museum September 5, 2002. They were made by Precision Signs of Austin. The signs are eight feet long and the word SPAM is illuminated at night.